D1646483

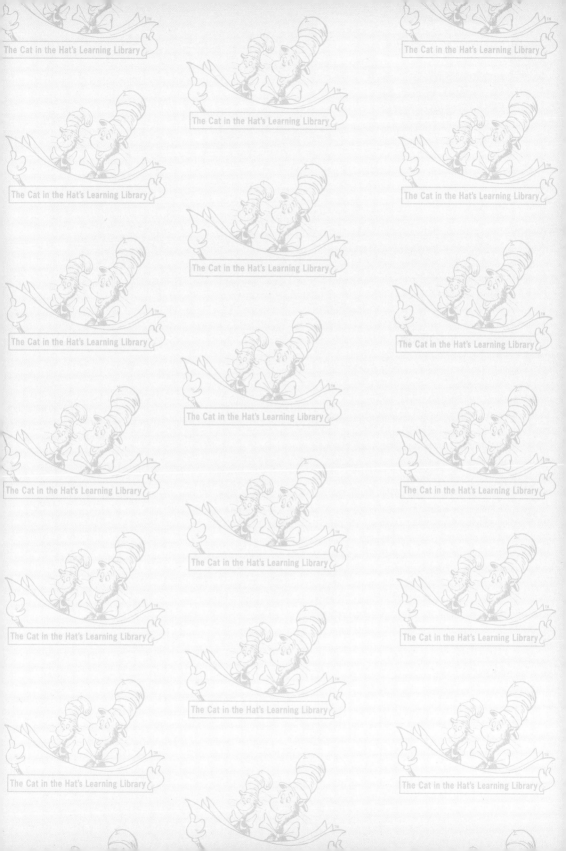

This question had Thing One and
Thing Two in a tizzy:

If the Earth's always spinning,
why don't we feel dizzy?

We don't feel the Earth
as it spins on its way
'cause we're spinning right with it
right now every day.

Next, here is Mars.
It's the colour of rust.
We sneeze here because
it is covered in dust.

Travel to Jupiter
and you will find
it is bigger than all
other planets combined.

Saturn has rings.

It's so light –

who would think?

It could float in an ocean
and not even sink!

A planet can have
satellites that surround it.
Uranus has lots of these
objects around it.

There are colours in space.

I will show some to you.

Neptune, you see,

is a beautiful blue.

If you lived on Pluto,
it would not be nice.
Some astronomers think
it is covered with ice.

It is chilly and cold
every night and all day,
for the sun's just a speck
in the sky far away.

An astronomer studies
what's up in the sky.
Thing Two wants to be one.
In fact, so do I!

We have seen all nine planets.

Now here is a trick

to remember their names

and remember them quick.

Say:

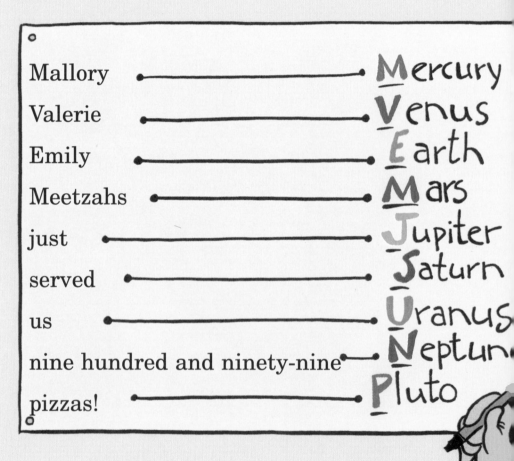

Mallory	**M**ercury
Valerie	**V**enus
Emily	**E**arth
Meetzahs	**M**ars
just	**J**upiter
served	**S**aturn
us	**U**ranus
nine hundred and ninety-nine	**N**eptune
pizzas!	**P**luto

The first letter of each
of these words is the same
as the first letter in each
of the planets you name.

Now here is a game
you can play in the skies:
connect all the stars
you can see with your eyes.

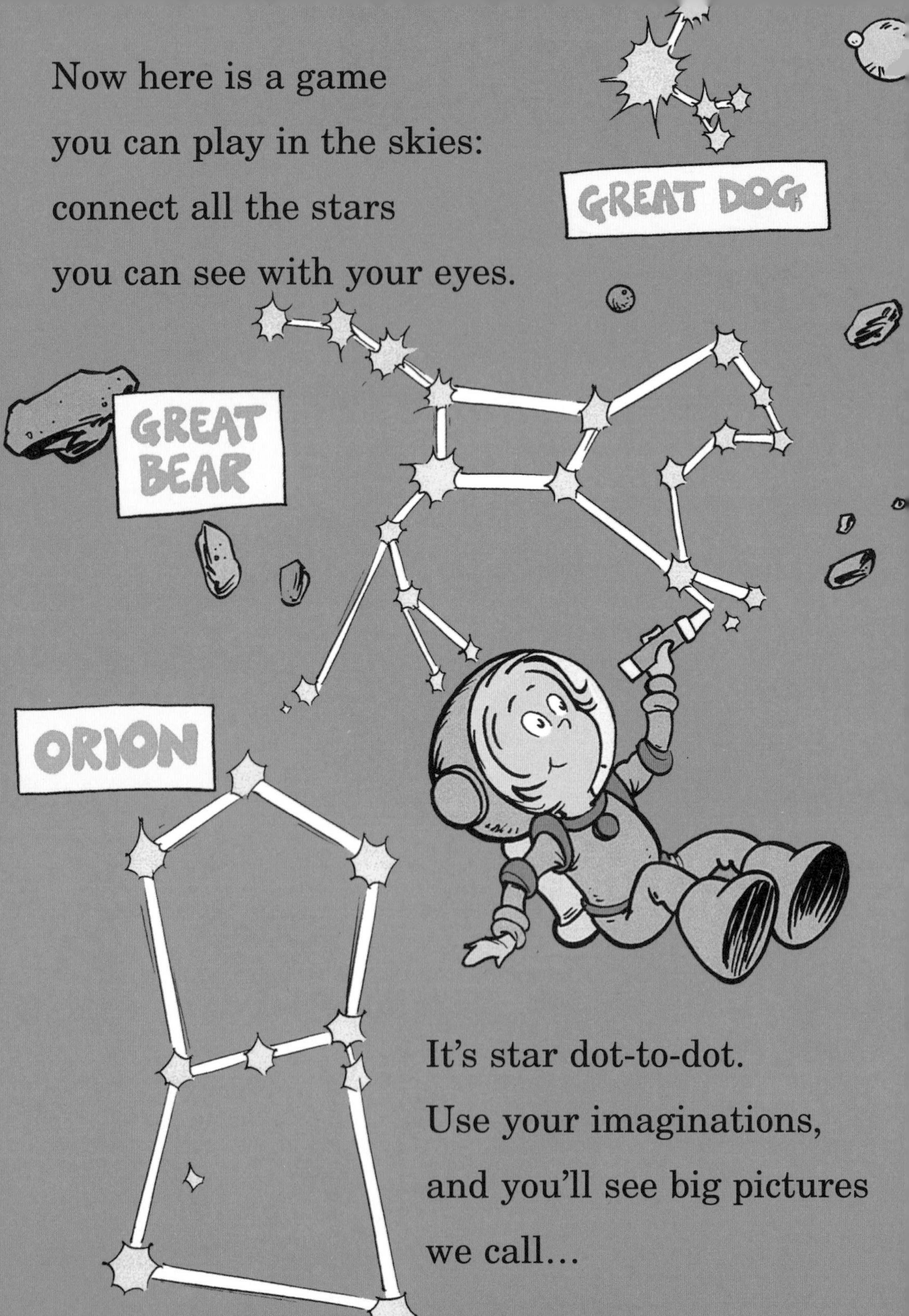

GREAT DOG

GREAT
BEAR

ORION

It's star dot-to-dot.
Use your imaginations,
and you'll see big pictures
we call...

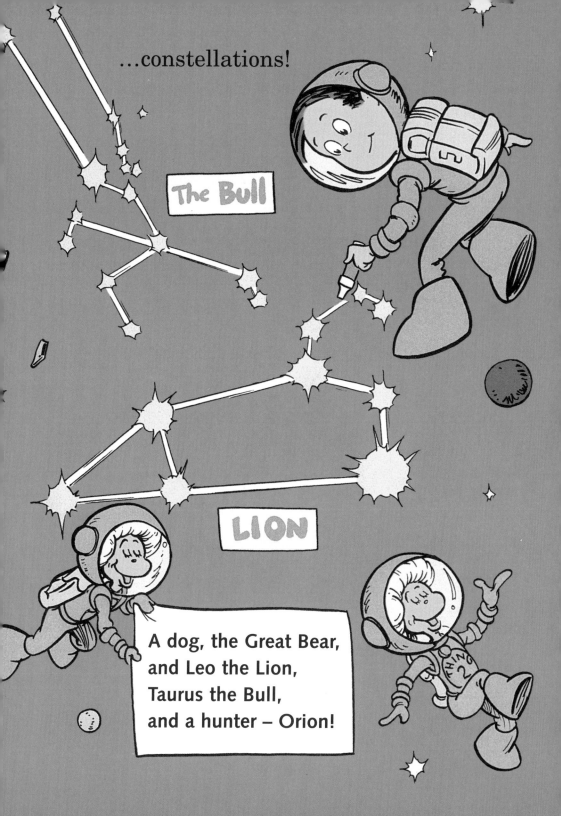

...constellations!

The Bull

LION

A dog, the Great Bear,
and Leo the Lion,
Taurus the Bull,
and a hunter – Orion!

A star in the sky
may look small, like a dot,
but it's really a big glowing ball,
and it's **hot**.

And there's one star by far
that's our favourite one.
We can't live without it:
the star called…

...the sun!

From the Earth it looks big.
There is one reason why.
It's the closest to Earth
of the stars in the sky.

But be careful and
never look right at the sun.
Your eyes would get hurt,
and that would not be fun.

How big is the sun?
We just heard
right this minute
a million of our Earths
could all fit right in it.

Oh, look at the time!
We must go very soon.
But first we must take
a quick look at the moon

The moon does not shine
in the sky in the night
but, like a big mirror,
reflects the sun's light.

The universe is
a mysterious place.
We are only just learning
what happens in space.

So I brought you a present!
To look in the sky –
just put this telescope
up to your eye.

Oh dear, I must go
fly back up to the stars
and take Things One and Two
out to dinner on Mars.

But there's lots to discover,
and it might be you
who looks up in the sky...

and finds something
that's new!

GLOSSARY

Astronomer: A person who studies the planets, stars, sun, moon and other heavenly bodies.

Constellation: A group of stars that form a pattern in the sky that looks like a picture.

Satellite: A natural or man-made object that moves around a planet.

Solar system: The sun and all the planets that move around it.

Telescope: An instrument that uses lenses to make faraway objects appear closer.

Universe: Everything that exists, including the Earth, the other planets, the stars and all of space.

FOR FURTHER READING

Star Boy's Surprise by Jana Hunter. This deceptively simple science fiction story about a boy who lives on a star, explores ideas of friendship and understanding. Ages 4+ (978-0-00-718613-6)

Let's Go to Mars by Janice Marriott. This unique persuasive text takes the form of a fictional holiday to Mars, presenting factual information about the red planet. Ages 4+ (978-0-00-718615-0)

Buzz and Bingo in the Starry Sky by Alan Durant. Buzz and Bingo find themselves in Outer Space trying to help a lost alien find its parents. Ages 5+ (978-0-00-718630-3)

INDEX

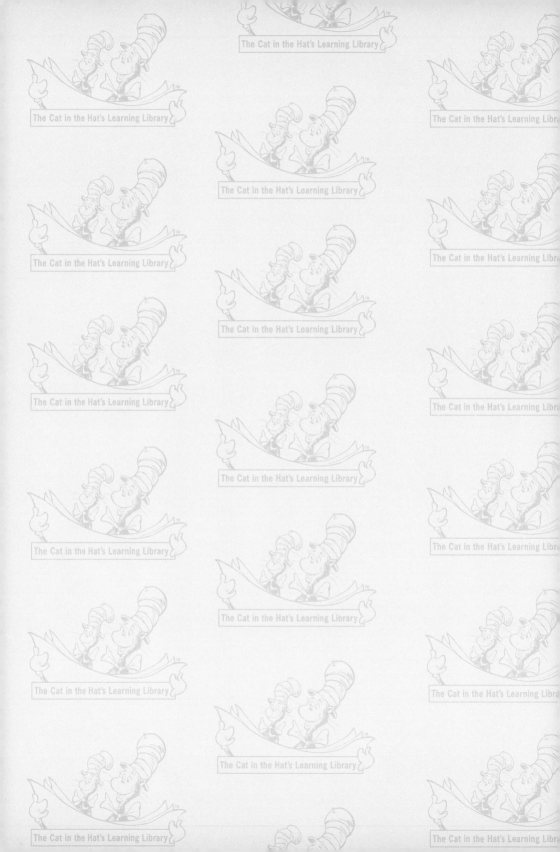

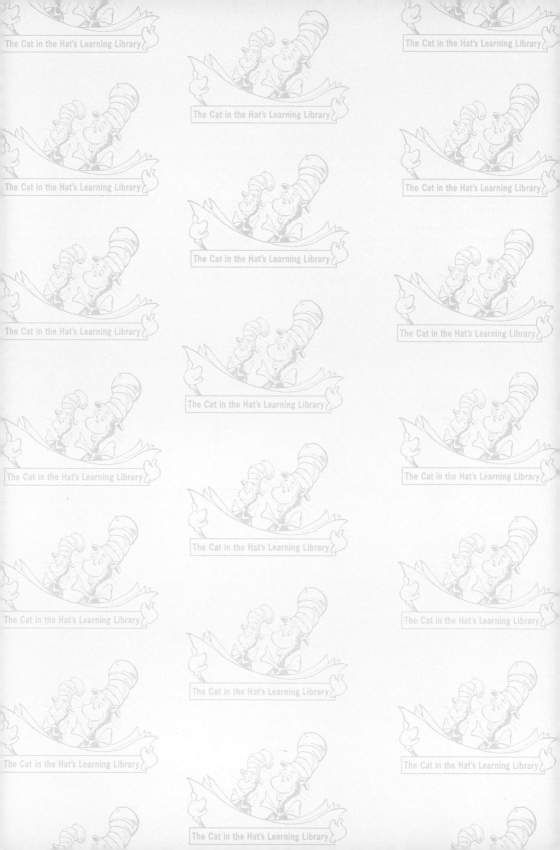

If you love The Cat in the Hat then look out for these great titles to collect:

OH SAY CAN YOU SAY WHAT'S THE WEATHER TODAY

WOULD YOU RATHER BE A TADPOLE?

MY OH MY A BUTTERFLY

I CAN NAME 50 TREES TODAY

MILES AND MILES OF REPTILES

A GREAT DAY FOR PUP

CLAM-I-AM!

A WHALE OF A TALE!

THERE'S NO PLACE LIKE SPACE!

OH, THE PETS YOU CAN GET!

IF I RAN THE RAIN FOREST

INSIDE YOUR OUTSIDE!

FINE FEATHERED FRIENDS

OH, THE THINGS YOU CAN DO THAT ARE GOOD FOR YOU!

IS A CAMEL A MAMMAL?

WISH FOR A FISH

OH SAY CAN YOU SAY DI-NO-SAUR?

ON BEYOND BUGS

OH SAY CAN YOU SEED?